# ZOO ANIMALS

by
Tessa Board

HAMLYN

LONDON · NEW YORK · SYDNEY · TORONTO

# ACKNOWLEDGEMENTS

*Black and white*
Toni Angermayer 56 (bottom), 58; Philip Arnold Photography 31, 37 (bottom); Barnaby's Picture Library 16 (bottom); Jen and Des Bartlett 22 (bottom), 26 (top), 26 (bottom), 27, 37 (top), 49 (bottom), 52, 53 (bottom), 54 (bottom); John R. Brownlie 53 (top); Camera Press 62-63; Central Press Photos 9 (top), 30 (bottom), 40 (bottom); A. Devaney 54 (top), 59; Fox Photos 9 (bottom); Gulliver Photos 48; Ingmar Holmasen 23, 30 (top), 49 (top), 61; Keystone Press Agency 10, 16 (top), 33, 45, 57; Russ Kinne 19 (bottom), 60; Leonard Lee Rue 55, 56 (top); Pictorial Press 19 (top); Popperfoto 44, 50, 51; S. C. Porter 22 (top); W. Suschitzky 36; Joe van Wormer 18; Zoological Society of London 2-3, 4, 11, 13, 14, 40 (top), 41.

*Colour*
Jen and Des Bartlett 24 (top), 35 (right), 39 (bottom); Jane Burton 17; Keystone Press Agency 28 (bottom); Russ Kinne 29; Okapia Frankfurt 28 (top); Eric Parbst 20 (top); Photo Researchers 34 (top left), 34 (right); Popperfoto 32; Masood Quarishy 20 (bottom), 25; Syndication International 34 (bottom); Terry Whitham 35 (top); Z.F.A. 38, 47; Zoological Society of London cover, 21, 24 (bottom), 35 (bottom left), 39 (top left), 42, 43 (top), 43 (bottom), 46 (left), 46 (right).

First Published 1971
Second Impression 1971

Published by
The Hamlyn Publishing Group Limited
London · New York · Sydney · Toronto
Hamlyn House, Feltham, Middlesex, England
© Copyright The Hamlyn Publishing Group Limited 1971
ISBN 0 600 34817 2
Printed by Litografia A. Romero, S. A., Santa Cruz
de Tenerife, Canary Islands

Most big cities have a zoo, and most children enjoy visiting their zoo as often as they can. Children and adults go to the zoo to see wild animals at close quarters – animals like lions, tigers, bears and monkeys which, most probably, they will never see in the plains or jungles or mountains which are the animals' natural homes. There are strange and exotic animals, bright and plain ones, gigantic and tiny ones to be seen. The zoo is a wealth of colours and patterns, of sounds and smells and textures. Each visit brings new excitement as well as the chance to see old and familiar friends. The zoo is also a place of education, and on each visit interesting new facts about the habits of the animals can be discovered. In addition to being a place for enjoyment and learning, it is also an ideal place in which scientists can study the structure, behaviour and diseases of animals.

Wild animals have been kept in captivity since at least the beginning of written history. The early rulers of Greece, Rome, Egypt, China and many other places kept private menageries for personal enjoyment and prestige, but often the animals were treated badly. In England a large collection of wild beasts, including lions, bears and elephants, was kept at the Tower of London from Henry III's time until 1832. Louis XIV of France collected his animals on one site at Versailles and planted trees, shrubs and flowers between the cages; he was probably the originator of the zoological *garden*. After the French Revolution the collection was moved to the Jardin des Plantes in Paris and was opened to the public from 1793. This collection inspired the naturalist and explorer Sir Stamford Raffles to create a similar display in London, and from his idea the famous 'Zoological Gardens' in Regent's Park were born in 1828. Soon zoos were being built all over the world. At the last count there were at least 800 public zoos in the world.

In modern zoos everything possible is done to keep the animals healthy and happy. At the same time they are kept in such a way that they can easily be observed.

Zoos display their animals in a setting as near to the animals' natural environment as possible. Penguins, seals, otters and polar bears are provided with pools in which they can swim and keep cool, and some zoos have underwater viewing windows for the public. Antelope, deer, giraffes and other hoofed animals are given large paddocks in which they can move freely. Chimpanzees, monkeys, coatis and squirrels have cages with trees and wire for climbing. Birds are kept in large flight cages with branches and bushes in which they can nest. Burrowing animals such as marmots and gerbils are exhibited in cut-away burrows so that their underground activities can be observed. Nocturnal animals, which are most active at night, are shown in red light or dim light so that during the day zoo visitors can watch them when they are most alert. Delicate animals can be kept in special cages where conditions such as light and temperature can be controlled carefully.

Zoo animals are kept, wherever possible, in pairs or family groups, or larger social groups. Sometimes different kinds of animals can be kept in the same enclosure. The cages or enclosures are separated from the public by moats which cannot be jumped, or by fences which cannot be jumped or climbed, or by glass which cannot be broken. These barriers are important for keeping the public at a safe distance from the animals, for even the most placid-looking zoo animal may suddenly decide to bite or scratch a hand pushed into its cage! But the barriers are also important to the animals themselves, because they represent the limit of the animals' territory. All animals tend to occupy only a certain area in the wild and do not wander freely. Without any such boundary, the animals would feel insecure and nervous with so many potentially dangerous humans around. In the same way your home is your 'territory', and you would not feel right with just anybody wandering in. The animal's territory ends with a fence or a moat, and he cannot go any farther, unlike animals in the wild. But he does have a number of very important advantages over his wild relations. Zoos offer protection from predators and rivals, from hunger and thirst, from disease and injury, and from dangers such as fires or hunters. As a result of all this, zoo animals are usually far healthier than their relatives in the wild, and tend to live much longer.

Animals arrive at the zoo in a number of different ways. Some are acquired as gifts and these range from unwanted pets like bushbabies and monkeys, which even the zoo may not have room

---

Giraffes, when kept in a spacious enclosure like the one on the opposite page, can run freely. In zoos animal families like the polar bear and cubs at right are kept together as much as possible.

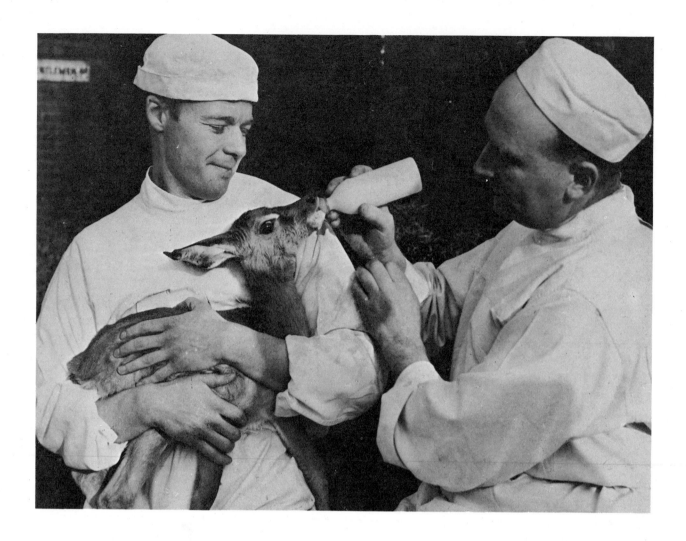

for, to a bear or lion from a head of state. Other animals arrive by
chance, such as an escaped parrot, or an abandoned fox cub,
which someone finds and brings to the zoo. Many animals are
bought from animal collectors and dealers in foreign countries.
Experienced locals collect the wild animals, feed them, prepare
them for the journey and fit out a special packing case for their
trip. Most journeys today are by air and the animal can be trans-
ported from its native country to the zoo in just a few hours. On
rare occasions a zoo sends out a special expedition of its own to
collect a particularly fascinating animal. Some animals are
acquired as parts of deals or exchanges between zoos or with a
foreign wildlife department. One zoo, for example, may have an
extra pair of pumas, and arrange to exchange them for a hippopotamus.

The most important way for zoos to acquire new animals is
by breeding them. Young animals are always an attraction, and

Orphaned impala (above) and lion cub (opposite page) are being
bottle-fed by zoo hospital staff.

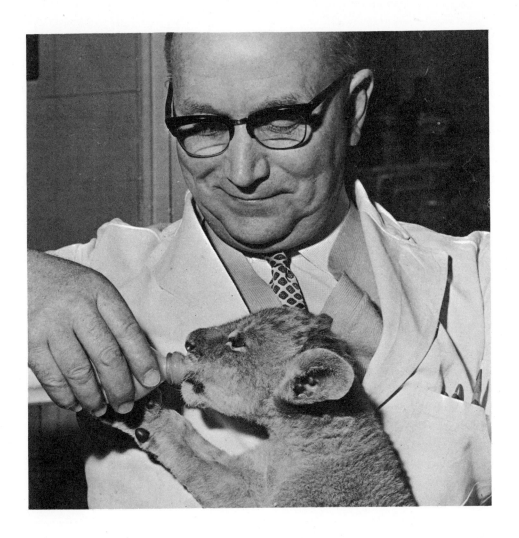

surplus animals are useful 'currency' for any zoo, to use in trading for other animals. But far more important is the fact that zoos do not have to keep taking animals out of the wild when building up a collection.

Zoo-born animals are a sort of reserve and can be vital to the survival of a species which is becoming extinct. Many animals are in serious danger in the wild, because they have been killed in great numbers by hunters, or because their habitats have been destroyed when farms, or cities, or roads have been built. Some of these animals breed well in zoos, and so can be preserved for many years to come. These rare animals include the tiger, the Mongolian wild horse, the pygmy hippo and the Hawaiian goose. Zoos are also making special attempts to breed other rare animals such as the mountain gorilla, the Galapagos tortoise and the Indian rhino, which are faced with extinction in the wild. Zoos can provide special areas for these animals to breed and rear their young with all the care and protection of experienced zoo staff at hand. Some kinds of animals are alive today only because they have been preserved in zoos. Pere David's deer and the wisent or European bison are extinct as wild animals, but luckily have been safeguarded in zoos, and individuals born in zoos have been sent to their original countries.

Animals born in a zoo get very special attention. The mothers and babies are housed in isolation cages where they can get all the food, warmth and quiet they need. If a mother will not raise her own baby, then it may be fostered by another animal, or reared by a keeper. Hand-reared babies have to have special diets, and round-the-clock attention by experienced staff. Animals born and reared in zoos provide zoologists and vets with excellent opportunities to study their growth from birth to maturity, which can rarely be observed in the wild. Animals born in the zoo have a special advantage over those born in the wild, for they are protected from dangers during a most important part of their lives. This is the time when they must leave their mother to fend for themselves. In the wild many animals die at this stage, but in the zoo there is no danger from starvation or from predators.

Animals in the zoo are grouped into houses or sections, and each section has a staff of keepers. The keepers are responsible for preparing the food for the animals, keeping the house clean, and keeping a close watch on the health of their charges. A keeper's day starts early. He arrives and greets the animals, then sets about cleaning out the cages and public areas, preparing the animals' breakfasts and providing fresh bedding and fresh water. When the visitors arrive he is kept busy answering questions and patrolling the houses. Then there is more cleaning up and food preparation in the afternoon and evening before the keeper is able to leave. Sometimes a keeper may have to stay at the zoo all through the night looking after a sick animal.

A zoo's shopping list is enormous. The plant-eaters such as rhinos, hippos, antelope and cattle require huge quantities of hay, grain and vegetables and smaller amounts of other items each day. In one day an adult elephant can eat 100-200 pounds of hay, plus root vegetables such as carrots and potatoes, locust beans, cabbages, grain, bread, apples, minerals and salt. A giraffe will eat about 30 pounds of clover hay, and also carrots, cabbages, oats, biscuits, fruit and minerals. Lions and tigers each eat about 10 pounds of beef steak each day, enriched with vitamins, and occasionally whole chickens and rabbits. Polar bears like fatty meat and are given 15-20 pounds a day, and bread, fish, carrots and cabbages. Brown bears eat both meat and vegetables; one large adult may eat 10 pounds of meat, 5 pounds of fish, 5 loaves of bread, and additional fruit and vegetables each day. An adult gorilla will eat 30-40 pounds of mixed fruits and vegetables, milk, bread and eggs a day.

The monkey house, small mammal houses and bird houses of the zoo will have the most varied food bowls to make up. Monkeys eat a mixture made up from some of the following: fruit, milk,

hard-boiled eggs, canned dog food, peanuts, bread and vitamins. The bird house will have many kinds of seeds and fruits, and vegetables, meat, fish, dried flies, shrimps, sugar water, and many other items from which to make up individual food bowls for each bird. As can be imagined, there are large stores of dry foods in each zoo, as well as enormous refrigerators for fresh food.

Many big zoos have their own hospital where young animals and sick animals can get proper care from vets. A zoo hospital is rather like an ordinary one for humans – with white-coated veterinary surgeons and animal nurses watching carefully over the patients – except, of course, that the patients are in isolation cages rather than beds! The zoo hospital staff also carries out routine treatment such as trimming nails, claws and hoofs, extracting teeth, and attending to minor wounds. Newly acquired animals from the wild first go to the hospital, where they

---

Manicures, pedicures, or a good brush-down – it's all part of the keeper's work (above).

are examined for parasites and diseases, before being placed on exhibition.

Many zoos have a special children's corner. Here some animals that make good pets, such as rabbits, mice, guinea pigs, tortoises and hamsters, can be stroked and fondled. Other pets such as terrapins, polecats, grass snakes, budgerigars and goldfish are also exhibited, and children can learn from special labels or the zoo staff how these pets can be kept in the home. There may also be sheep, goats, tame deer and antelope, pigs and calves to be seen. Young zoo animals – a brown bear, for example, or a young monkey – can be petted by the visitors. There may be an exhibition of chicks hatching out of eggs in a special incubator, or a viewing panel into an animal nursery, where zoo babies can be watched as they are cared for by their animal nurses and keepers. Most children's corners have animal rides, on Shetland ponies or camels, and pony trap or llama cart rides.

The following pages show a few of the unusual and exciting animals zoos have to offer. It is hard to imagine a nicer way of spending your time than looking at, and learning about these fascinating animals.

---

Riding high on the camel's back – not in the deserts, but at the zoo! (above).
The hippopotamus (opposite page) is being given a special tit-bit by his keeper.

Elephants are the largest and heaviest living land mammals. A large male African elephant could stand over 10 feet high at the shoulders and weigh over 6 tons. The easiest way to distinguish between African and Indian elephants is by the size of the ears, which are much larger in the African elephant. The babies, opposite page, below, are Africans. An elephant's skin dries quickly in the sun and is sensitive to insect bites, so elephants like to bathe frequently, as the baby on the left is doing, and then cover themselves with mud or sand, as below.

Bears are many people's zoo favourites, with their heavy, furry bodies, short round ears and flat-footed waddling walk. Although they are the largest of the carnivorous (meat eating) group of mammals, bears will in fact eat anything from meat and fish to insects, fruits and, of course, honey. The European brown bear (right) has been driven from most of its former range in the wild, but the American black bear (below) is protected in several National Parks. The great white polar bear of the Arctic (opposite page, below) has a slender build ideal for diving and swimming, and feeds mainly on seals in the wild.

20

Lions and tigers are the biggest and most impressive of the big cats. A large male lion (opposite page, below), with his shaggy mane, certainly deserves his title of 'King of the Beasts'. Unlike other big cats, lions live together peaceably in family groups called prides, sharing their food, and looking after the youngsters. The lionesses do most of the hunting for the pride. Lions are the least bloodthirsty of all the big cats and usually kill only what they need to eat. Lion cubs, like the ones on the left, are spotted at birth, but the spots disappear as they grow up. Tigers (below) range over parts of Asia, often living in or near forests, where their boldly striped coats provide good camouflage when stalking or resting. The tiger has good senses of sight, smell and hearing to detect its prey, and strong teeth and claws to kill it. It is the most powerful of the big cats when roused, but in the zoo it likes nothing better than a good snooze!

22

Wild dogs are runners and hunters with strong legs and keen senses of smell and hearing. They can follow a scent trail as easily as a man follows signposts. The wolf (below) is an extremely cunning animal which works with others in a pack to bring down its prey. The jackal (opposite page, below) hunts in packs by night and sometimes follows larger carnivores to feed on the remains of their kills. It makes a loud howling or yapping noise. The little arctic fox (left) lives in the Far North. It has a brown coat in the summer, but in the winter a paler coloured coat grows for camouflage in the snow.

All cats are adept at leaping from a sitting, standing or running position, and landing on their prey with claws outstretched and jaws wide open. The slender caracal lynx (left) is a good runner and hunts all sorts of animals, including gazelle, sheep and goats. It can be recognised by its striking ears with black tufts. The little leopard cub, opposite page, below, will grow into an excellent climber; leopards can drag heavy kill into the trees. The cheetah (below) is the fastest animal on land and can sprint at well over 60 m.p.h. for a short while. It is built for speed, with its small head and ears, lithe body and powerful legs.

Many animals are most active by night, seeking their food under cover of darkness. We call these nocturnal, and in some zoos we can watch them in special houses where it is like night during the day. The slow loris (directly below) and the slender loris (right), have short ears and no tails. They grip the branches tightly with their hands and feet and creep cautiously up on their insect prey. The large eyes help them to see in the dim light. The bushbaby or galago (bottom of page) has large ears, a long tail, and long hind-legs used for jumping. Its fur is beautifully soft and silky. Bushbabies feed on insects, fruit and eggs.

When exhibited in zoos, the amiable bear-like giant panda (opposite page, below) is a great favourite. This rare creature lives in inaccessible mountain regions of China, and feeds mainly on bamboo. A close relative, the attractive red panda from the Himalayas (left) is an excellent climber and spends much of its time in the trees. Raccoons (below) are related to the pandas, and live in North America. They hunt in water for fish, frogs, mussels and other water animals, and they also eat birds, eggs, insects, nuts, fruits and berries – a truly varied diet!

Camels and llamas have been associated with man for thousands of years. Some two-humped, or Bactrian, camels (opposite page) still live wild in the Gobi Desert, but most are domesticated and used mainly as pack animals. Camels are extremely hardy animals. Their humps contain a reserve of fatty tissue on which they live when there is nothing to eat. Wild relatives of the camels live in South America, and the llama (below) is a domesticated animal descended from them. Llamas and camels can survive days without water, but in the zoo they drink every day.

The giraffe (left) is the tallest living mammal, and can grow to over 19 feet high! It uses its long body to reach up to the leaves and shoots of acacia trees in the wild. The giraffe's coat is marked with brown blotches for camouflage. The shape and colour of the blotches vary in different parts of Africa. Giraffes are good runners, but cannot swim. Bold dark stripes mark the coat of the zebra, also from Africa. Zebras live in large herds on the open plains, and are often preyed upon by lions. But in the zoo the little foal and its mother, below, know no danger from predators.

By far the most colourful animals are the birds, and at the zoo we can see birds from all over the world. Zebra finches from Australia (left) are often kept as cage birds. The crowned crane from Africa (below left) is majestic in its golden head-dress. The blue-and-yellow macaw from South America (right) has a beak strong enough to crack Brazil nuts. The little owl of Europe (below) hunts by day and by night for small animals. The peacock from India and Ceylon (opposite page, bottom left) has the most beautiful display. The greater flamingo from Africa (opposite page, bottom right) feeds most elegantly with its head held upside down.

Chimpanzees are probably the most intelligent of the apes, and in zoos the young ones are often trained to take part in tea parties (opposite page, below) to show off their skills. They learn to eat from a bowl, pour milk or sweet tea from a pot, and drink from a mug, although their table manners are not always perfect and they may get up to mischief when the keeper's back is turned. Chimps can also learn to ride bicycles, sweep floors, wash up, and many other things. A young chimpanzee (below) has a flesh-coloured face, hands and feet, but as it grows older the skin darkens. Chimps have expressions just like people. They can move their mouth, lips and eyes to express emotions such as friendliness or fear. On the ground chimpanzees usually walk on all-fours with their hands folded so that they lean on their knuckles, but they can also walk upright, as at right. An adult chimp is more powerful than the strongest man, and weights about 150 lbs.

There are well over a hundred different kinds of monkey in the world. Little marmosets and tamarins live in large groups in the trees in South America, feeding on insects, fruits and leaves. Some are very colourful, like the golden lion marmoset (right). Some other New World monkeys, such as the capuchins, spider monkeys and woolly monkeys, have prehensile tails which can be used to grasp branches.

The monkeys of the Old World usually have long tails, but these are never prehensile. Many Old World monkeys have cheek pouches to store food, and patches of bare skin on the buttocks which may be brightly coloured as in the case of the sacred baboon (below). Baboons always move on all-fours and live in rocky regions. De Brazza's monkey (far right) is a forest-dwelling guenon monkey. The patas monkey (opposite page, below) spends most of its time on the ground.

The apes have a special fascination because they are man's nearest relations. Like man they have a well-developed brain and no tail, and they can walk in a more or less upright position. Gibbons (left) live almost entirely in the trees, swinging along at great speeds, using their very long arms. Orang-utans (opposite page, below) are also tree dwellers, but they swing or walk more carefully through the branches. At night these red-haired apes build nests of branches and leaves. The gorilla (below) is the largest of the apes. Not surprisingly this mighty creature has no natural enemies, and is in fact not dangerous unless provoked. It prefers to spend its day quietly feeding on fruits and vegetables, usually on the ground.

Antelopes are generally graceful hoofed mammals of slender build which can move at great speeds. In the wild they live in a variety of places, from deserts to swamps to forests. Their horns vary as well – some are short, others are long, some are straight, some are lyre-shaped, and some are twisted. The greater kudu (below) is a stately antelope whose horns may make two and a half open spirals. The horns of the male blackbuck (right) may have up to five turns. Some female antelopes also bear horns, but the female blackbuck is hornless. She is also paler in colour than the male. Deer differ from antelopes in that they have branched antlers. The antlers, borne generally only by the males, are shed each year and regrow. The sika deer (opposite page, below) is a small deer and its horns have four 'tines' or points. In the summer this deer has a chestnut coat spotted with white, but in the winter the coat darkens.

Many animals are disappearing in the wild because man kills them for his own gain or for sport, or destroys their natural surroundings for plantations or towns. For these animals the zoo is a haven where they can live and breed unharmed. Zoos may help to prevent some animals from complete extinction, as in the case of the European bison and Pere David's deer which can no longer be found as truly wild animals. The rare proboscis monkey (right) is a very odd-looking mammal with its exaggerated nose which becomes even more bulbous in an adult male. This picture shows the first proboscis monkey ever born outside Borneo, at San Diego Zoo, in California.

The beautiful okapi (below), with its velvet-like coat, is a shy and secretive antelope from the Congo, where its future is very uncertain. Fortunately the okapi breeds successfully in several zoos, where it becomes very docile.

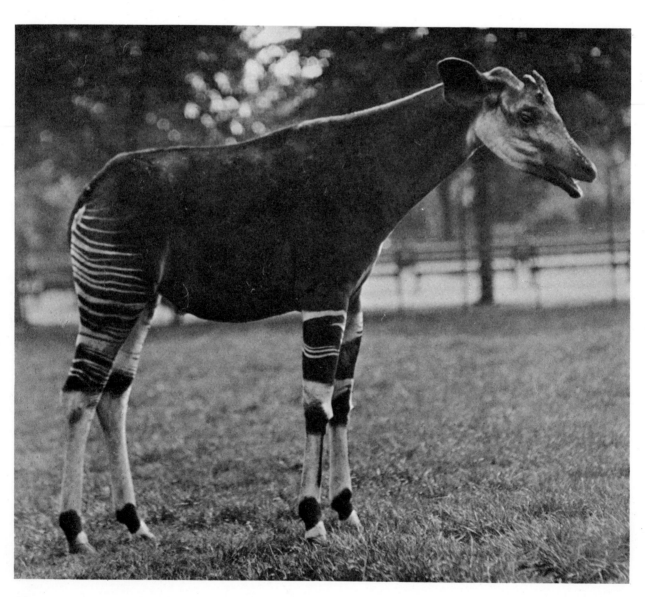

One of the greatest thrills when visiting a zoo is to be able to touch and stroke the animals. This is not possible in the main zoo, where the wild animals may scratch and bite, but many zoos have a special Children's Corner. Here are young and tame wild animals, and domesticated animals, all ready to be petted by the young visitors. Special friendships are made, as below, although sometimes the animals can get too friendly, like the goats at the far left!

As well as the collection of rabbits, hamsters and guinea pigs, there may well also be rides in a llama cart, or on a pony (left).

Marmots and porcupines are rodents and have curved front teeth used for gnawing. The prairie marmot (left) is an excellent burrower and makes extensive underground tunnels. It feeds on grass, roots and seeds, stopping frequently to stand up and look around. The crested porcupine (below) has long quills which it raises in defence. The quills are only loosely attached to the skin, and fall out easily, but they cannot be shot out like darts.

The elephant shrew of Africa (bottom of page) is a small insectivore with a long sensitive snout which searches for insects, and long hind legs for hopping around.

Kangaroos and other marsupials are born at a very early stage of development and most spend the first few months of life safe in their mother's pouch where they feed on her milk. Even when the young 'joey' is able to run around on his own he still makes a dive for the pouch when he gets tired. The one on the left went in head first. The koala (below) is another marsupial. It has soft fur, large ears, bright eyes and a black nose, and is often copied for toys. However it is not often seen in zoos partly because of its rather fussy diet of certain eucalyptus leaves. Koalas were once so widely hunted for their fur that they were nearly exterminated.

In tropical parts of the world insects are abundant and some mammals have become adapted for feeding on them. These mammals have powerful digging claws to break down ants' and termites' nests, long noses to probe into the nests, and long sticky tongues to pick up the fast-moving insects. The pangolin or scaly anteater (below) has a protective shield of scales and can roll itself into a ball, hiding its soft parts. The aardvark (opposite page, below) has a strange name meaning 'earth-pig', and digs large burrows. The echidna or spiny anteater (right) belongs to the group of egg-laying mammals called monotremes.

Domestic cattle, pigs and sheep have many wild counterparts in Africa and northern parts of the world. The Barbary sheep (left) is a very hardy animal which lives in the mountains of North Africa. Both males and females bear the curved horns. The young wart hog (opposite page, below) is in the pig family. When older its large head is covered with warts, and the tusks are longer and curved. The heavily built Cape buffalo from Africa, below, has just enjoyed a mud bath, which is cooling and keeps the skin in good condition. This breed of buffalo can grow to be five feet tall at the shoulder and weigh 1,750 pounds.

In a happy zoo, some of the enclosures will contain mothers and their zoo-born youngsters, growing up in a safe and comfortable environment. If the little one has difficulty in keeping up with its mother she gives it a ride, as with the little vervet monkey at right, clinging to its mother's belly. The common opossum (below) is a marsupial, and the youngsters spend 100 days in the pouch before moving round to mother's back. The sealion pup (bottom of page) is almost helpless at birth, but has to learn to swim quickly, since it cannot be carried around by its mother.

Rhinoceroses and hippopotamuses have thick skins and little hair, and next to the elephants are the largest land mammals. The black rhinoceros from Africa (left) has a pointed upper lip, used to pluck leaves, twigs and long grasses. The small eyes indicate a poor sense of sight, but rhinos have an acute sense of smell. They can be very dangerous and often attack for no apparent reason. The hippopotamus (below) paddles along rivers and lakes in Africa, peacefully scooping water plants with it cavernous mouth. It can rest on land or in the water, submerged for periods of up to 30 minutes. At night it forages on land among the reeds.

Although mammals are mostly land animals, and birds are animals of the air, some kinds from both groups have become specially adapted for a watery life, and taken advantage of the food resources of the oceans. Seals, sealions and walruses are all clumsier on land than they are in the water although, of course, they cannot breathe under water. The walrus (below) is not often seen in zoos. It can grow to 10 feet in length and weigh 3,000 pounds. The King penguin (right) has a streamlined shape ideal for diving and swimming after fish in the cold southern seas. On land it waddles or hops about, or toboggans on the snow.